Chapter 1

Who Lives At Your House?

Can you list all the living things that live with you?

You might list the pets who share your home. Perhaps you have a cat, or a bird, a dog, or some rabbits?

You might list the animals that you have seen in your back yard. Most back yards have birds, such as blackbirds, pigeons or sparrows living in them. You may have some birds that are special to your country or your area.

You may have seen other animals. In warm places, many back yards have lizards living in them. In some places, you may even have snakes living in your back yard!

WHO SHARES YOUR HOME?

Written by
Leigh Crummisch

HORWITZ
MARTIN

Contents

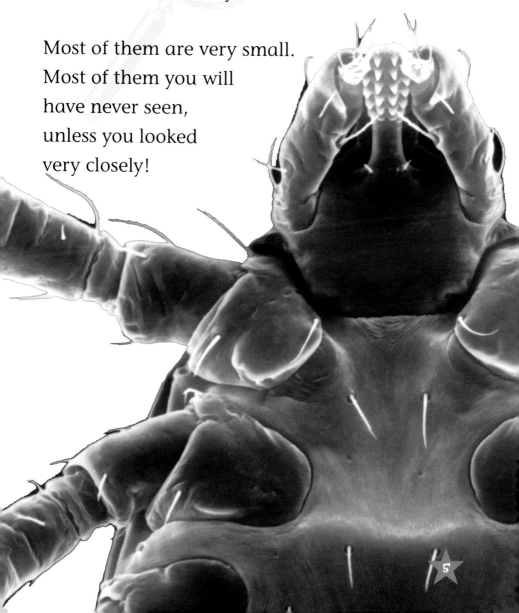

You may think that you could count all the animals that share your home. You would have to think again! There are many other living creatures that share your home.

Most of them are very small. Most of them you will have never seen, unless you looked very closely!

Do you think there are five, ten or twenty animals who share your home? Do you think there could be a hundred? Do you think there could be a thousand?

Think some more!

There are *millions* of living creatures in every home.

Think about which animals might be living in your home right now.

Can you think of an animal which is smaller than you, smaller than a dog, a cat or a bird?

Have you ever seen ...
... a mouse in your house?

Chapter 2

A Mouse In Your House

Mice are rodents. This means they have special teeth to gnaw, or chew, things. They are good at gnawing because they have sharp, square teeth that keep growing.

Mice build nests out of chewed-up paper, straw and other materials.

If you ever see a mouse inside your home, you can be almost sure there are more.

Mice breed quickly. When a mouse is only 42 days old, it is ready to breed. Every six weeks, a female can have about seven baby mice. Within four or five months, one mouse family can grow to about 140 mice.

Squeak!

Mice come into your home to find food and warmth. They build their nests in walls or under floors. Mice can squeeze through tiny ... or spaces. If you don't want to share your ... mouse, you must block up all the ... use can come in.

You might think mice are cute. But they can carry diseases that make people very sick. They also leave their droppings behind them.

People use traps and poisons to try to get rid of mice.

Cats, who might already share your home, are very good mouse-catchers. Farmers keep cats to help stop mice from eating their crops.

Miaow!

Fleas are small jumping insects that can live on mice. Fleas can carry germs, so be careful!

Can you think of another animal, smaller than a mouse, which might live in your home?

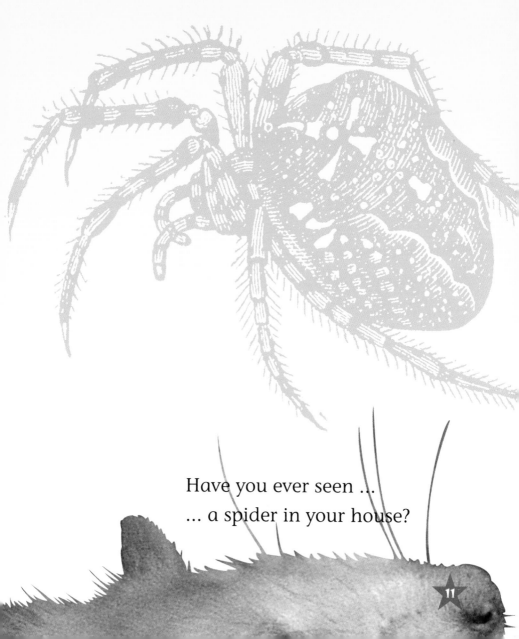

Have you ever seen ...
... a spider in your house?

Chapter 3

Ipsy Wipsy Who?

*D*oes anyone in your house scream when they see a spider?

Before you decide to get rid of that spider, think about how it might help you.

Nearly all spiders have venom, or poison. They use it to weaken their prey, usually insects.

Huntsman spiders are a type of spider that grow very big. They often scare people. Their fangs are big, but their venom is weak. They don't often bite people, but they are very good at catching insects.

Other smaller spiders come into homes and spin webs in corners and near ceilings. They also feed on insects, such as flies, mosquitoes and beetles.

Did you know …?

Spiders are not insects. They have eight legs.
They are classified as arachnids.

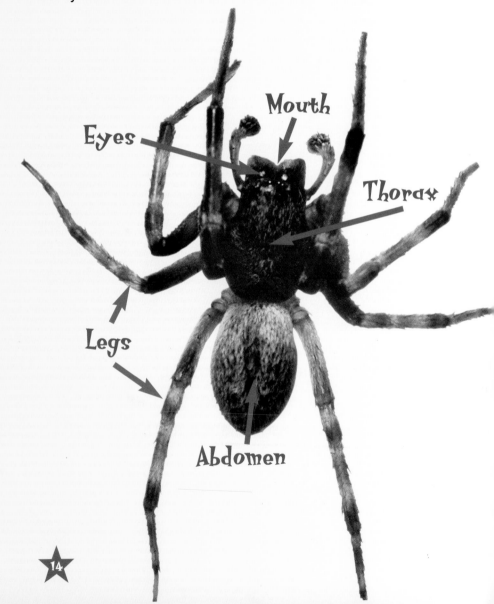

Eyes

Mouth

Thorax

Legs

Abdomen

Some animals that share our homes are welcome. Some are not!

A fly is not welcome, as it carries germs.

Have you ever seen ...
... a fly in your house?

Chapter 4
Buzz!

Flies spend most of their time near garbage and manure, so they carry many germs.

Always cover food, so flies can't land on it. Wipe benches and tables clean before putting food on them. People can become very sick from the germs carried by flies.

Flies are insects. They have six legs. They have one pair of wings. A fly can sense movement, using compound eyes that have hundreds of lenses.

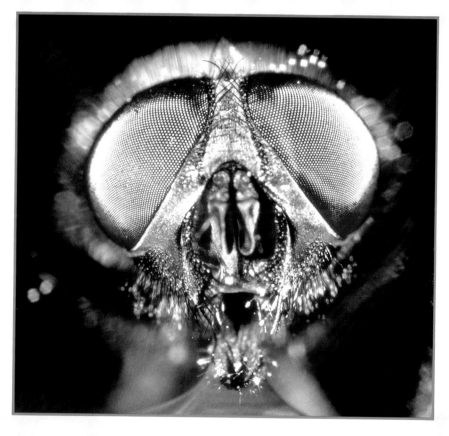

A blowfly is much bigger than a housefly. It makes a buzzing noise. There are more than 90,000 types of flies!

You might hear a mosquito buzzing around your home. Did you know that a mosquito is a fly, too?

Female mosquitoes are blood-sucking flies with biting, sucking mouthparts. A mosquito is twice as heavy after she has finished sucking blood. Mosquitoes can pass germs from one person to another.

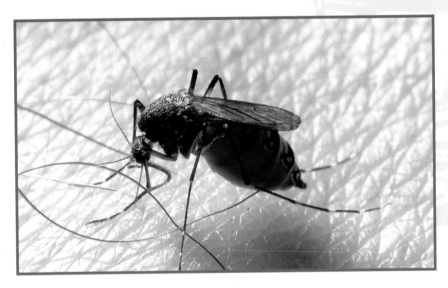

Mosquitoes breed in water. If you have a pond, or puddles around your home, look for mosquito larvae.

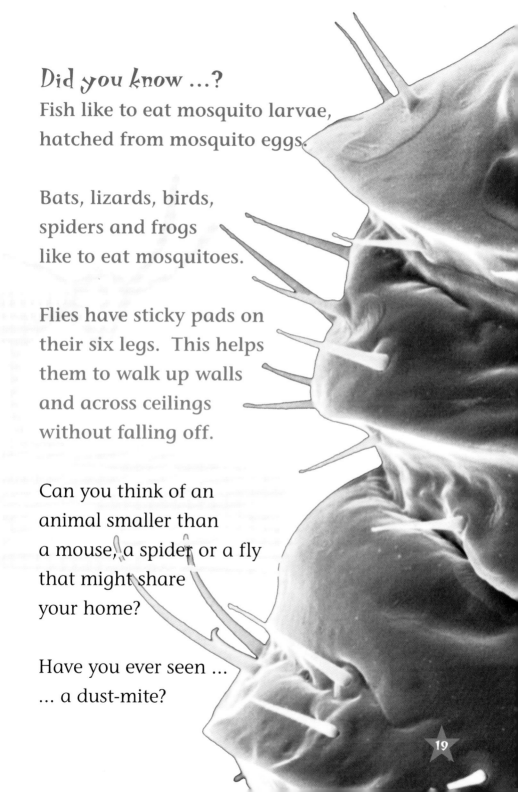

Did you know ...?

Fish like to eat mosquito larvae,
hatched from mosquito eggs.

Bats, lizards, birds,
spiders and frogs
like to eat mosquitoes.

Flies have sticky pads on
their six legs. This helps
them to walk up walls
and across ceilings
without falling off.

Can you think of an
animal smaller than
a mouse, a spider or a fly
that might share
your home?

Have you ever seen ...
... a dust-mite?

Chapter 5

You Might See A Mite!

You might see a mite (but you probably won't)!

Some creatures that share your home are there to stay. Dust-mites are tiny creatures, about one-third of a millimetre long. If you look at one under a microscope, you will see this:

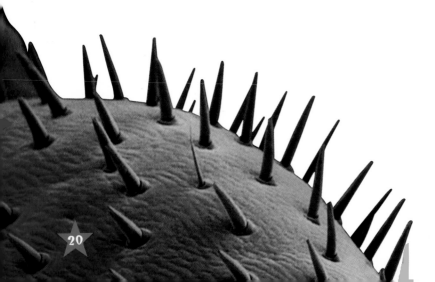

Millions of dust-mites live in your home. Their favourite places are close to you, especially in your bed! Dust-mites like to feed on tiny bits of dead skin. Every day, humans shed millions of tiny bits of skin. Much of the dust in your home is made up of human skin.

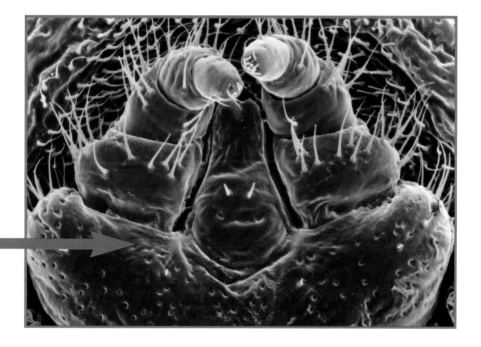

Changing bed sheets and vacuuming will get rid of many dust-mites, but lots will be left behind. They keep eating and breeding, so you probably won't get rid of these visitors.

Dust-mites are classified as arachnids, together with spiders. The life cycle of a dust-mite is two to three weeks, from egg to adult.

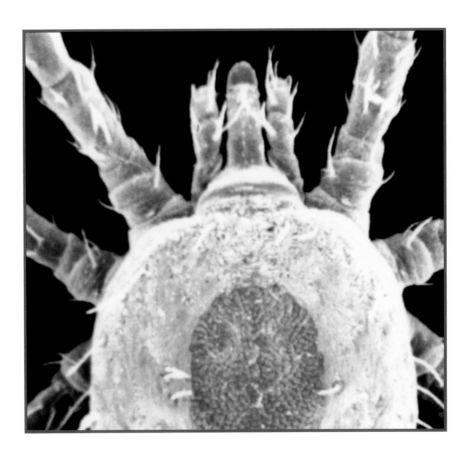

As well as the mice, spiders, flies and dust-mites sharing your home, there are many other creatures. They are all your neighbours!

Chapter **6**
Who Else?

Say hello next time you see some ants, bees, beetles, fleas, moths, snails, silverfish or cockroaches.

Most animals depend on other animals for food, shelter or protection. Many of the animals you share your home with depend on you—whether you like it or not!

Index

Glossary

breed
To have babies.

classified
Put into groups.

compound eyes
Eyes with lots of lenses.

creature
An animal.

fangs
Sharp teeth.

larvae
The young of an insect, like a caterpillar.

lenses
The clear parts of the eye that light passes through.

manure
The waste from animals.

prey
Something that is hunted for food